A Life In Full Bloom

The Story & Paintings of

Olivia Bennett

Published by
International Art Publishers, Inc.

Olivia Bennett and International Art Publishers would
like to gratefully acknowledge our co-publishers without
whom this book would not have been possible:

DR. JODI ARAGONA LUKACSA - DR. TOM LUKACSA

DR. YOUNG LEE - DR. KYONG LEE

DR. EARTHA DAVIS - MR. MICHAEL COVERT & SER TECHNOLOGY CORP.

BILLY & DIANNA TERPSTRA - TOM & PATTY STRAWMYER

MS. CHRISTY SCANLAN - ROBERT & CRYSTAL BURDETTE

DICK & MARCELRADUENZEL - DR. MARY BOURAS

MR. SAM HERSHEY - KEVIN & KORLA ST. CYR

DR. GREG JUNG - DR. HILARY HANSON-JUNG

ROBERT & KATHLEEN FAIR - MS. SHARON GOODLIN

INTERNATIONAL ART PUBLISHERS' WISHES TO EXTEND OUR DEEPEST THANKS TO JERRY & VERDA TOLER,
JENNIFER BIRDSALL AND ERNIE LEWIS FOR ALL THEIR YEARS OF DEDICATION AND SUPPORT.

International Art Publishers, Inc.
23121 Antonio Parkway
Rancho Santa Margarita, CA 92688

ISBN 0-9724568-0-5

Library of Congress Control Number: 2002111695

1st printing 2002

See more of Olivia's paintings at: www.oliviabennett.com

Visit International Art Publishers, Inc. at: www.intartent.com

A Life In
Full Bloom

The Story & Paintings of

Olivia Bennett

Foreword

At the age of eleven Mozart composed the opera *"Apollo and Hyacinthus"*. Composers like Schubert and Mendelssohn all composed masterworks at early ages, and performers like Chopin, Saint-Saëns, Hummel, Clara Wieck, and Yehudi Menuhin had all given public performances by the time they were 11 years of age. How can an eleven year old compose such works? Or perform them? How can a child musician play an instrument at a level that should have taken years to master? To me, the answer is simple: it is a gift!

Twelve year-old Olivia Bennett is a child painter the way Wolfgang Mozart was a child composer. In fact, when I first gazed upon Olivia's canvasses, I remember thinking, *"Watching Olivia paint is like watching Mozart compose!"* Like the great composer, Olivia possesses skills and techniques that should have taken at least half a lifetime to develop. Hers is not talent, hers is a great gift!

All prodigies are rare but visual art prodigies are probably the rarest (musical prodigies appear on the scene a little more frequently). Some say this is because the sense of hearing develops in human children, perhaps even in the womb, long before the sense of sight

Yet no concession to Olivia's youth should be made in judging her art. If it is to be considered legitimate, it must bear up under the same scrutiny as any adult painter. Does the art tell us something about ourselves? Does it instill within us a sense of wonder? Of awe? Are we richer for having gazed upon its image? In Olivia's work, we find all of that and more. Hers is more than purely art; it is a gift unfolding on the canvas. We cannot view her paintings without feeling a great sense of renewal, of hope, of optimism. Yes, leave it to a child of twelve to show us what is possible if we simply believe strongly enough.

From a technical perspective, her work holds up just as well. Her palette is explosive and vibrant as the almost kaleido-scope-like quality of *"Chrysanthemum"* demonstrates. Her brush strokes are bold enough to capture the necessary patriotic emotions in *"Let Freedom Bloom"* yet gentle enough that one fears a strong wind might send a petal from *"Crystal"* on a fanciful flight. Her ability to use light is brilliantly demonstrated in *"Michele's Rose"* where the viewer almost feels compelled to look behind the canvas to identify the source of its back lighting.

You are about to see on the following pages an ability, a gift, almost impossible to believe and certainly impossible to explain.

-- Ben Valenty

A Life
In
Full Bloom

The Story of
Olivia Bennett

PART ONE

Michele's Story

August 1994

I'll never forget the hopeless, terrified feeling I had when I was told that my five year-old daughter might have leukemia.

We had just moved back to Salt Lake City, Utah from Grand Rapids, Michigan. My husband, Matt, had finally found a job after being off work for six long months. Olivia had taken the move very hard. She had cried for days when we finally said goodbye to her close friends in the neighborhood. Even though Olivia wouldn't be five for a couple of weeks, she seemed wise to the world. Because she was so bright and precocious, many people assumed she was much older.

Olivia had been extremely worried when her dad was unemployed. She had felt it was her job to comfort her dad and she had wanted to know everything that was going on at all times. I would tell her to go and play and let daddy and mommy be concerned with finding a job, but she wouldn't do it. Olivia was happy for her dad the night he received the job offer but it also tore her up emotionally. She knew it meant moving and she was crushed. I could never have guessed it would affect her so much.

Olivia's fifth birthday party in Salt Lake City brought a smile back to her face. She was surrounded by grandparents, aunts, uncles, and cousins. She had lots of presents and lots of love. They all knew how hard the move had been for her and they wanted her to be happy. Things seemed to be going great. We had found a new home and would move in before Christmas. Olivia would start kindergarten in two weeks time, and her little brother, Michael, would be going to preschool. We were looking forward to getting settled and starting over. And then our world was shattered!

I found a new doctor close to our home and had taken Olivia in for her required kindergarten physical. I assumed she was perfectly healthy. She was acting like herself, but I noticed the glands on her neck were swollen. One protruded like a small grape, but I really didn't think much of it at the time.

Our new pediatrician, Dr. Lynch, gave her a physical and the necessary finger-stick to check for anemia. When the test came back, he told me that Olivia was anemic and would need more blood-work done at the hospital the next day. I felt confused but agreed to go. A few days later, I got a call from Dr. Lynch that devastated us. He said Olivia had either Epstein Barr virus or Leukemia. Matt and I were shocked! Just hearing the word Leukemia terrified us. Dr. Lynch said we had to wait one week and have another test done to see how that blood compared to the first test. That week crawled painfully by. Matt and I lie awake at night crying and praying that we wouldn't lose our little girl. She was so bright and so precious to us. We felt lost and alone in our pain.

The evening of September 1st, 1994, Dr. Lynch called us at home and confirmed the worst - Olivia indeed had cancer and would be admitted to Primary Children's Medical Center the very next morning to start chemotherapy.

On September 2nd, Olivia received blood-work, a bone-marrow aspiration, and a spinal tap. The test revealed Acute Lymphoblastic Leukemia or ALL. She would need to start chemo immediately and would be treated for 26 months. We admitted Olivia to the hospital and began what would be the longest and hardest days of our lives. It was incredibly difficult to see her go through so much and at times we felt helpless. I remember wishing I could take away her pain.

Olivia told me she hated the "bow and arrow" that the doctors did to her. She was referring to the bone marrow aspiration - one of many more to come. One day at the hospital, she whispered in my ear, *"Mommy, I hate being five!"*. I always knew she was a special girl. I just didn't want her to be this type of special.

Three times a week, I would take Olivia to the hospital's Hem/Onc clinic for her chemotherapy treatment. She had had a temporary pick line inserted in her arm that led to an vein in her heart for the chemo injections. She also received a shot in her leg and every other week, Olivia had to endure a bone marrow aspiration or spinal tap. It was so difficult for Olivia, but she was extremely brave through it all. She focused and concentrated hard and held very still for the tests. The doctors and nurses were very impressed with the way she handled herself. I found that she needed to know everything that was happening to her and she would ask questions before each procedure. Most children respond best with distraction, but Olivia had her own way of coping and was upset if we tried to interfere with her concentration. Her bravery amazed me.

Three weeks after the start of chemotherapy, Olivia's hair started to come out by the handful. I cried and cried because she really had started to take on the look of a child with cancer and the reality of it sunk in deeper. She had had pretty, wavy blond hair and it was hard for me to hide my feelings from her. She was sad but handled it fairly well. Olivia started to save her hair in a sandwich baggie. When she had collected it all, she put some if it in the back yard so the birds could use it in their nests. She loved animals and this made her happy. We collected it from her pillow and added to the baggie every day.

As the weeks and months rolled by, Olivia seemed to get worse and worse. During much of the time, she was so sick that she could only spend most of each day curled up on the couch. She started to become weak and had trouble walking. I had to carry her up and down the stairs to her room and if I needed to take Michael to preschool or pick him up, I would wake her and carry her to the car.

Olivia's few remaining strands of wispy hair finally fell out and she was completely bald. She tried in vain to hide her head with an assortment of hats. When we went places, children would point and say, *"Mommy, why is that girl bald?"*. Naturally, it crushed Olivia and she asked me to buy her a wig.

We found a wig shop and purchased one that looked similar to the color of her natural hair. She loved it and felt like a princess when she wore it. We were willing to do anything to help her feel good about herself again.

Olivia had surgery to remove the pick line from her arm and to implant a central catheter line in her chest. This more permanent line would hopefully last the full two years and its purpose would be to draw blood and administer the chemo.

It was around this time that I noticed how intent Olivia had become about coloring, drawing and painting, which seemed to be the only activities that took her mind off the pain and nausea. I made it a point to keep ample art supplies on hand. Whenever Olivia felt strong enough, she would sit at the kitchen table and create her art - sometimes for hours on end.

Almost before it began, even this one joy in Olivia's life was threatened. One of the drugs Olivia received through her "line" was called Vincristine. It was and still is an important cancer drug. In Olivia's case, the Vincristine would have a rare and debilitating side-effect. Two months after her first vincristine treatments, I had noticed that she had suddenly become weak in her upper body. Her fingers were curled into a claw-like position and she was unable to accomplish the one thing that gave her the most comfort - holding her drawing pencils and paint brushes. Even when she was relaxed or sleeping, her fingers remained curled.

During Olivia's chemotherapy, I kept a journal to help me through the long months. I knew it would be important for Olivia to someday read and remember.

Journal Entry - January, 1995

"Tomorrow you start another round of chemo. The doctor says this
one is going to be extremely intense. You've just finished six weeks
of physical therapy to try to get some mobility back into your hands. It
must be working a little because you're once again holding a paint brush
and creating such beautiful works of art. We have six more weeks of
therapy, this time concentrating mostly on your fingers.

On our next visit to Primary Children's, the doctors confirmed that Olivia was having a bad reaction to the Vincristine. We started Olivia on physical therapy and that helped return strength to her hands. She slowly regained enough strength to be able to draw and color, and she spent hours at the kitchen table creating note cards, pictures, and Valentines.

Journal Entry - February, 1995

"You actually seemed to be better the last couple of weeks but all of a sudden,
you've really gone downhill. You can't walk at all any more. I don't mind
carrying you, but I'm now five months pregnant. You have no energy
and you're nose bleeds once in a while, yet you keep on smiling and
you have a great attitude. You tell me you love me and it breaks my heart.
I wish your dad and I could take some of the pain from you...."

Olivia wanted desperately to go to school and since she had missed the start of kindergarten, Michael's preschool teacher invited her to come to his class whenever she felt well enough. The school started to send workbooks home with Michael with assignments for Olivia to complete. She couldn't get enough. We knew her favorite assignments involved coloring and drawing and she never tired of it. She drew the rainbow fish, clowns, and pictures of rainbows, and carefully dated and signed each one. The stacks of paper grew. We bought her paints and paper and she lost herself and her worries in her artwork.

One day, Olivia entered one of her paintings in the hospital's Camp Hobe cancer camp contest and was thrilled when it was chosen for the camp's t-shirts. It would be the first of many contests she would enter and win. Painting became her passion and her obsession. It eased the long days of painful procedures and fulfilled her desire to create.

At night she would be resting peacefully and I would check on her before going to bed myself. Sometimes I couldn't tell if she was breathing, and her face was so pale it would scare me. I would kiss her gently hoping she would move so I could be sure. I was afraid she might just slip away, though the doctors assured me it wouldn't be like that. They said "I would know" and gave me no other explanations. She was still so beautiful with her big blue eyes and short downy-soft hair that was finally growing back in. She was such a gift to her family and she fought her disease with all of the strength she had.

And she smiled and tried to keep a positive attitude through it all.

Journal Entry - May, 1996

"Dear Olivia,

Sometimes I look at you, so still, sleeping in bed at night, and it makes me think scary thoughts. We just assume we'll never lose you to cancer. You look so pale and still that I walk over and kiss you in hopes that you'll move a bit and reassure me that you're okay. I mean,I know that you are, but it makes me think. And makes me appreciate having you. In a few months you'll be seven. I guess I feel very lucky to have you. You've changed so much in just two years. It is incredible. You've always been mature for your age, but you've really grown mentally in the last two years. I just thank God every night for letting us keep you. You are so incredibly special to me (us, I guess - Dad feels the same way). I admire your strong-will, courage, and the growing artist in you. I pray that you never give up your talents. They will always be with you - I just hope you continue to thrive on your artwork and don't turn your back on your talent".

At long, long last, the months of pain and worry appeared to be coming to an end. After two years of non-stop chemotherapy, Olivia's cancer was in remission and she felt good enough to start school at Waterford in September of 1995. The following year, her art teacher, Mr. Huff, thought Olivia demonstrated talent in art and suggested we enroll her in Petersen Art Center in Salt Lake City. Olivia began her lessons in February of 1997.

Her first painting at Petersen was of an eagle flying. It was incredible and we framed it. I started framing almost every watercolor she produced. We searched for art contests and entered her work. She received 13 first, second, and third place ribbons.

While in the second grade, her frog painting was juried into the Hogle Zoo contest where she competed on an adult level. She won first place in her division, for the state of Utah, in the Junior Federal Duck Stamp contest. She was in third grade and only nine years old at the time. From that moment on, painting became Olivia's passion.

PART TWO

A Career In Full Bloom

by Derek Partridge

In 1999, Matt's company transferred him to the Dallas area. For Olivia, the move to Texas meant a change of scenery from Utah's Wasatch Mountains. Soon after they arrived in Texas, Olivia discovered the nearby Fort Worth Botanical Gardens, where she would spend hours developing ideas for paintings. She found herself favoring the roses and magnolias for their bright colors.

In August of 1999, Olivia celebrated her 10th birthday and the beginning of her professional art career when a woman saw one of her paintings and insisted on buying it for $50. Olivia had heard about an art festival in Southlake, Texas (near Dallas) where local artists are able to exhibit their works. Olivia applied for entry and was accepted by the jury. To their astonishment, Olivia sold 20 paintings. The following year, she sold 32 paintings at that show!

Olivia next applied to enter the much larger Red River Revel Arts Festival in Louisiana, which has attracted as many as 200,000 visitors from the surrounding five states. The Bennett's were surprised and delighted when Olivia was accorded the honor of being the first artist under the age of 25 (at just 11 years old) to ever participate in this prestigious event.

Shortly after Olivia returned from Louisiana, Michele got in touch with Melanie Singleton, the director of the Thurburn Gallery in Fort Worth. Melanie arranged to see Olivia's work and realized that it showed maturity far beyond her chronological age. Melanie offered to display Olivia's work in her gallery. The response was so strong that she was given a featured art exhibit at the gallery…. an undreamed of accomplishment for an 11 year-old.

A few weeks after Olivia's gallery exhibit, a neighbor showed Michele an article in a national magazine about a teen artist who had been completely unknown until being discovered by Ben Valenty, an art publisher specializing in child prodigies. Under Ben's guidance and management, the teen artist's career had already reached national status. Ironically, it turned out that Ben had also discovered (then) 10 year-old Alexandra Nechita and had been the driving force behind her career. Olivia had purchased

Alexandra's book, *Outside the Lines,* and had greatly admired her work. The article also pointed out that Ben would be in the Dallas area for an exhibit that week.

Michele learned that Valenty had an office in Southern California. She found the phone number and dialed. The receptionist told her that Ben was indeed in Dallas and promised to have him call Michele back. An hour later, Ben did call. Michele told him about Olivia and asked if they could meet with him while he was in town. Ben agreed and suggested that they meet at his hotel.

When Ben met Olivia and looked at her portfolio, he knew instantly that hers was a gift unlike any he had ever seen. *"As I was looking over her paintings, I remember thinking that this must have been what the person who discovered Mozart felt like."* Ben agreed to sign Olivia to an exclusive publishing and management agreement.

February 2002

Olivia waits in the library of Samuel Tucker Elementary School in Arlington, Virginia. The painting behind her, entitled *Let Freedom Bloom* nearly dwarfs her. She is nervous and fidgeting. In a few moments, she will meet the President of the United States and the First Lady. Olivia is at the school to be recognized by the President for selling limited edition prints of *Let Freedom Bloom* to raise funds for America's Fund for Afghan Children.

Applause breaks out as the President and First Lady enter the room. Mr. and Mrs. Bush immediately approach Olivia to offer congratulations. Both seem genuinely moved by the massive canvas of an American flag cradled by a single red rose. The President then escorts Olivia to the school auditorium where he is scheduled to deliver a speech.

"Today, we're joined by a special young lady from Texas. I wanted to single her out as someone who has done a little extra - not a little extra, a lot extra - for the fund to help Afghan boys and girls," the President tells a national television audience.

As soon as the President and First Lady have left the building, media video crews, newspaper reporters and photographers descend upon Olivia. For the next couple of hours, she patiently gives interview after interview. Finally she is whisked away for the ride to the airport, with a quick stop at the hotel to pick up her luggage. When she enters the hotel lobby, another media crew awaits her, this time from an ABC affiliate. She graciously does a quick interview and hops back into the car just in time to take a call from a producer from the Today Show. Arrangements are quickly made for Olivia to appear the next morning, via satellite, with Katie Couric.

It is almost 10:30 pm in Dallas when Olivia's plane arrives at the gate. The long day has worn her out although her smile is still ear-to-ear. Little does she know that more media crews are waiting for her at the baggage claim, hoping for interviews.

Olivia finally arrives home, well past her normal bedtime and she is due at NBC Studios early the next morning for her interview with Ms. Couric. She is still too keyed-up to sleep. She tells her Mom about an idea that came to her during one of the day's dozens of interviews. She bounds upstairs to her studio, covers herself in paint-splattered denim overalls and sets up a large canvas. She grabs a handful of paint tubes and begins mixing her magic formula once again.

Today, at the ripe old age of 12, Olivia's career has already reached superstar status. Demand for her original work has been astonishing. Fascinated by the images Olivia so deftly brings to life on her canvasses, collectors join waiting lists for new works, snapping them up as fast as she finishes them. In a matter of months, over 200 of Olivia original paintings have sold. Her limited editions sell even faster. Prices are rising, too. Two years ago, Olivia's paintings sold at her first show in Southlake, Texas, for $25 to $300. Today, her canvasses command up to $5,000 -$10,000 apiece and are expected to climb much higher. Indeed, single collectors have purchased as many as a half-dozen of her paintings at a time. Some say they are attracted by the youthful spirit her work portrays while others feel the paintings are inspirational and represent her victory in her battle with cancer.

Her first love is - and she says, always will be - the floral subjects. These are usually composed by combining the best features into one vibrant blossom on the canvas. Incredibly, she has recently been experimenting with abstract studies that are every bit as sophisticated and accomplished as the florals. Olivia has also taught herself to deftly switch from watercolor to acrylic to oils with equal virtuosity - an extremely rare feat. Today, fortunately cured of her cancer, Olivia considers that she definitely appreciates life in a different way than she would have, had she not endured her encounter with cancer - a common reaction from survivors of close calls with their own mortality. As Olivia and her painting skills continue to mature, a hardly surprising situation for a 12 year-old (even a child prodigy) Olivia's legions of admirers wonder what the future holds for her. While Olivia wisely considers she still has a great deal to learn about art, she hopes that one day her work will be considered important enough to be studied by other budding artists… an honorable ambition.

Michele's Last Journal Entry - December 3, 2000

*"I can't sleep. I'm tired yet I feel almost haunted by a
painting you made tonight. As you were finishing it,
I told you it was so good, it was almost scary. I looked
at it and I look at you and think, 'My God, who is
this person I'm living with?" Tonight's painting is of a
magnolia with dark shadows and green petals.
It is utterly fabulous. I wonder who is in your soul,
guiding your hand? An old master, perhaps? "*

A Life
In
Full Bloom

The Paintings of

Let Freedom Bloom

oil on canvas
48" x 60"

(created at age 12)

When I first heard the terrible news of the terrorist attacks
on September 11th, I felt shocked and horrified. I wanted
to create a painting to express my feelings. *Let Freedom Bloom*
is my tribute to the heroes, victims, and families who
lost loved ones that day. To me, the rose symbolizes
love, and the emerging flag symbolizes our nations healing.
It made me feel so terrific when President and Mrs. Bush
told me how much they liked *Let Freedom Bloom*.

Jodi's Rose

watercolor on arches paper
22" x 30"

(created at age 12)

My mom and I were driving home after an
art show in Louisiana and decided to stop
in Shreveport at the American Rose Center.
As I was walking through the gardens,
I noticed a particularly beautiful rose that
begged to be painted. When I completed it,
I decided to name it after Dr. Jodi Aragona,
because she loved it so much. Dr. Jodi
started collecting my art very early in my
career and now we're good friends.

Fellowship Rose

watercolor on arches paper
28" x 22"

(created at age 11)

I found *Fellowship Rose* at a really
beautiful botanical garden near where
I live. I wanted to show the flower as its
petals are opening to the rays of the sun.
It reminds me of how important it is
to always feel hope and optimism.

Tree Frog

watercolor on arches paper
9" x 11"

(created at age 11)

I begged my mom for years to buy me a
pet frog but she never gave in. When we
lived in Michigan, we had a pond near
our house. We would take nets and
buckets there to catch the cutest frogs to
take home. I still get excited when I find
frogs in Texas but since I can't keep them,
I have to settle for painting them.

Large Water Lilies

watercolor on arches paper
22" x 30"

(created at age 10)

I was at my cousin's wedding in Austin.
While I stood on a little arched bridge
I looked down and noticed a pretty pond
with beautiful white water lilies. One flower
caught my eye and I knew I had to paint it.

Reflections of Fall

watercolor on arches paper
22" x 30"

(created at age 10)

Mom & Dad used to take my brother Michael
and me up to the mountains above our house to look
at the pretty fall leaves. I would collect them
in a baggie and take them to school to
show my teachers and friends. The
colors were so pretty I had to paint them.

Sarah's Rose

watercolor on arches paper
22" x 30"

(created at age 11)

Mom thinks *Sarah's Rose* is so beautiful.
She loves the rich, deep, velvety petals.
She says she loves the way the petals
look soft enough to touch. I named it after
my little sister, Sarah, because I love her
so much... she is so special to me.

Karen's Violin

watercolor on arches paper
23" x 15"

(created at age 12)

Karen is one of my best friends.
She is 12 years-old, too. I am amazed
at she can play the violin so beautifully.
She told me that her violin is very old
and has a history of its own. Her music
inspired me to paint *Karen's Violin*.

Brandy

watercolor on arches paper
30" x 22"

(created at age 11)

As I was painting *Brandy*, I realized
how much the colors of this rose reminded me
of the rock formations in Southern Utah.

Enchanting

watercolor on arches paper
30" x 22"

(created at age 11)

Enchanting is as much a mood as it is a flower. To me, a flower can be mysterious and beautiful at the same time. I love the way the petals curl around each other until they reach the center of the rose. This rose is really *Enchanting!*

Japanese Rose

watercolor on arches paper
22" x 28"

(created at age 10)

A Japanese rose is different than other roses.
They have the most beautiful petals. In certain
light, the petals almost become translucent. They
are so magnificent that I had to paint one.

Royal Dane

watercolor on arches paper
30" x 22"

(created at age 11)

I have never painted a floral quite like
Royal Dane. I think the vibrant colors
with the dark, rich background make it
stunningly beautiful. My mom has a
special place in her heart for this painting
and would never part with it.

Polka Dot Rose

watercolor on arches paper
16"x 22"

(created at age 11)

I don't know how I got the idea for
this painting. I wanted it to be different
than anything else I had painted. It
started out as black polka dots on
white paper. Then I painted the rose
around the polka dots, which was the
hardest way to do it. But I really had fun!

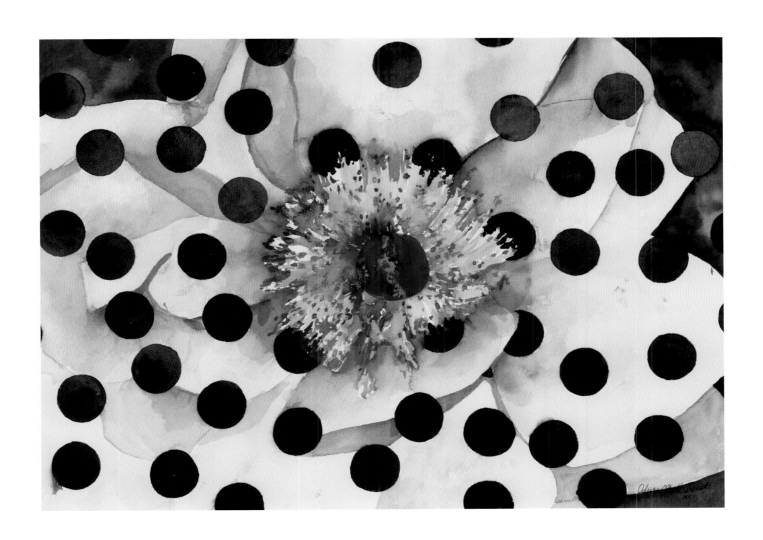

Jungle Birds

watercolor on arches paper
15" x 15"

(created at age 11)

I think Birds of Paradise are extremely "artsy-looking". I chose to paint these flowers with a leopard print background so it would make them look even more exotic.

Monet's Garden

watercolor on arches paper
22" x 30"

(created at age 12)

A friend of the family took a vacation
to France with her husband. She knows
I am inspired by flowers, so while in
France she visited and photographed
water lilies and flowers in Monet's garden.
She brought back photos for me to
paint from. She said I would have loved
Paris and my hope is to some day go there.

Wine Country

oil on canvas
24" x 36"

(created at age 12)

When I think of *Wine Country*, I think
of the magnificent countryside with the
vineyards growing so beautifully. I couldn't
wait to paint a "wine country" scene.

Wild At Heart

watercolor on arches paper
30" x 22"

(created at age 11)

Wild at Heart was an extremely fun painting
for me to do. I displayed it at a show in
Louisiana and I got several comments from
local people who wondered if I was a
Louisiana State Tiger fan. Even though
it wasn't my intention, I was able to find an
"L", "S", "U" in the painting. Also, it was
painted in Purple & Gold, the school colors.
What a coincidence!

Sea Turtle

watercolor on arches paper
11" x15"

(created at age 10)

I painted *Sea Turtle* just for fun. I always enjoy
painting lots of different living creatures so this
gave me a chance to try something a little different
but still challenging. I was very happy with
the way this painting turned out.

Crystal

oil on canvas
30" x 40"

(created at age 12)

Sometimes when the sun hits the petals of a
flower just right, it looks like they are made
of a very thin and delicate crystal. So I tried
to capture that feeling with this painting.

Heliconia

watercolor on arches paper
15" x 15"

(created at age 11)

I think heliconias are one of the most
beautiful plants. Until recently, I had
never actually seen one. I think they
are exotic looking. I added a zebra print
to give this one a wild look and I loved
the way it turned out.

Chrysanthemum

watercolor on arches paper
29" x 30"

(created at age 11)

I loved doing this painting because it was
so challenging. It's kind of like a prism
of colors that are all separate yet run together. This
one was fun, exhausting and rewarding.

My Grandfather

pencil drawing
12" x 10"

(created at age 9)

When I had my first art show in Texas,
I sent my paintings to Utah to be framed.
When they were ready, my grandfather
refused to take a chance on shipping them
back to us in case they got lost or didn't
arrive in time. So he drove them all the way
from Salt Lake City to Dallas in one day.
He was always wanting to help people
and it meant a lot to me that he would
drive that far to get them to me safely.
I used high school graduation
photo for this portrait.

Wine & Roses

watercolor on arches paper
23" x 15"

(created at age 11)

I think still life paintings are so beautiful,
especially when they're done by a great
artist. I had fun setting up this composition and
painting it. It was really a challenge and
I enjoyed seeing the painting progress

Birthday Card

oil on canvas
30" x 24"

(created at age 12)

Birthday Card is another of my favorites
because it was one of my first abstracts.
As I was painting it, I decided to include
my birthday to give it special meaning.

816 First Ave

water color on arches paper
23" x 15"

(completed at age 10)

My parents were traveling through Arkansas
when my mom pointed out a beautiful, old
brick house to my dad. She asked him to pull
over and she took several photographs of it.
She said she loved the many brick colors and
wrought iron. It was so stately. Every so often
she would leave the photos laying around and
hints that she wanted me to paint it. I finally did
and it's vey special to her. I put my birthdate
in the address to make it ours.

Sunshine Sunflower

oil on canvas
40" x 30"

(created at age 12)

To me, when I see a sunflower, I think
of sunshine. Even the center of the
sunflower looks like the sun. I love seeing
sunflowers growing wild in the field!

Wood Duck

watercolor on arches paper
9" x 12"

(created at age 9)

When I was in the 3rd grade, I entered this painting in the Junior Federal Duck Stamp competition. I borrowed a wood duck and studied it very carefully because I wanted the painting to be just right. It took me days to complete the painting and it won 1st place. I got a huge blue ribbon.

Morning Dew

watercolor on arches paper
8" x 8"

(created at age 10)

I'm very proud of this painting because
my goal was to capture the morning
dew drops on the petals of a flower
and that's pretty hard to do. I think
this one turned out really nice!

Coliseum

watercolor on arches paper
22" x 14"

(created at age 11)

With this painting, I was experimenting
with painting structures. I wanted to
do something classically Roman so what
better subject is there than the Coliseum?

Dawn

watercolor on arches paper
18" x 15"

(created at age 11)

I am so amazed at the gift Michelangelo had.
I read about how he was given many
commissions by the de Medici family including
their tomb. I was fascinated by one of the sculptures
Michelangelo did for the De Medici tomb and
that inspired me to create this painting.

Fuchsia

watercolor on arches paper
11" x 13"

(created at age 11)

Fuchsias are such delicate little flowers.
When my grandmother lived in Seattle,
she had hanging baskets on her front
porch that were full of fuchsias. They
were bright pink and purple..... so pretty!

Helen's Magnolia

watercolor on arches paper
17" x 15"

(created at age 11)

We have a small magnolia tree in our front
yard that blooms with big beautiful magnolias.
The flowers don't last very long but if I'm
quick, I can paint them before they wilt. I
named this one after the lady who owns it.
Her husband bought it for her as a Christmas gift.

Wildflowers & Lemons

watercolor on arches paper
14" x 15"

(created at age 9)

I had fun painting this because of all the
delicate little flowers in the arrangement.
In Utah, the wildflowers bloom in the mountains
and this painting reminds me of those.

Splash of Wine

watercolor on arches paper
22" x 30"

(created at age 12)

A few months ago, I started getting very
interested in abstract works by masters
such as Braque, Picasso and Kandinsky.
I love modulating shapes and forms in
an artistic way and then adding a
vibrant color palette.

In My Dreams

watercolor on arches paper
22" x 30"

(created at age 12)

I've always been fascinated with the effect
I get when I close my eyes and concentrate
on what I see. I can see so many shapes and
colors. This painting is the result of
what I can see when I close my eyes.

Golden Wings

watercolor on arches paper
30" x 22"

(created at age 11)

Golden Wings is one of my favorite paintings.
When I saw this flower, it looked as if
it could actually fly away if it wanted to.
I loved the way the colors turned out on this one!

Pretty Water Lily

watercolor on arches paper
22" x 30"

(created at age 11)

I saw this flower when I was looking
across a pond not far from home. It sort
of sat there by itself with dew drops on
it and around it. It was incredibly beautiful
so I remembered it and started painting
it as soon as I got home that day.

Michele's Rose

oil on canvas
40" x 30"

(created at age 12)

I was working on a painting of this large,
backlit pink rose. My mom came up to my
studio and absolutely fell in love with it.
I decided to dedicate it to her because
it's one of her favorites.

Stones

watercolor on arches paper
22" x30"

(created at age 12)

Stones reminds me of all the colorful stones
and gems jewelers use to make jewelry.
I love all the different varieties. When I
see this painting, I think of jewelry.

Olivia Bennett